Role-Play Revision for GCSE French

T. P. Murray

D1386921

CASSELL

To Roisin, Matthew, Daniel, Frances and Ellen

First published 1990 by Cassell Publishers Limited
Wellington House, 25 Strand, London WC2R 0BB, England

© Cassell Publishers Limited 1990

Reprinted 1992 (twice)
Reprinted 1993
Reprinted 1995
Reprinted 1996
Reprinted 1997

British Library Cataloguing in Publication Data
Murray, T. P. (Terry P.), *1948–*
    Role-play revision for GCSE French.
    1. Spoken French language
    I. Title
    468.3'421

ISBN 0-304-31869-8

Typeset by Litho Link Limited, Welshpool, Powys, Wales.
Printed and bound in Great Britain by
Cox & Wyman Ltd, Reading, Berkshire.

Contents

To the teacher and the pupil

I have selected the role-play situations and prompts in this book using my experience as a teacher of GCSE languages in a comprehensive school and as a Chief Examiner with a GCSE board. The material in this book covers the syllabuses of all the UK exam groups.

The role-play part of the oral test requires a lot of practice and it is not always easy to find prompts in English to practise on. It is for this reason that this book has been written. Each unit has been divided into three parts:

- Essential vocabulary.
- A list of English prompts.
- A list of suggested answers to those prompts
  (at the back of the book).

Needless to say, there is always more than one way of communicating an idea in a foreign language. I have selected the expression that I feel GCSE/Standard candidates will find easiest to remember and to use.

I suggest that the pupil approach each unit as follows. First, learn the vocabulary section. You will find that you will be floundering later on if you don't. Then, look at the English prompts. Don't try to work through a whole section. Take, say, five or ten prompts. See if you can answer them and then look up the answers at the back of the book to see how you fared. The book can be used for pair-work in class and is ideal for homework setting.

In your exam, you may have to express a feeling as well as communicate a fact. For instance, the prompt might say:

'Say that you do not agree and ask to see the manager.'

To cater for this, I have included a special section called 'Expressing your feelings'. In addition, there is a list of useful phrases, which will be valuable in many role-play situations.

Bonne chance!

Terry Murray
Head of Modern Languages, Edgecliff School, Staffordshire
Joint Chief Examiner in Spanish for MEG

Useful phrases

Où est . . .?	Where is . . .?
Pour aller à . . .?	How do I get to . . .?
A quelle heure est . . .?	What time is . . .?
A quelle distance est . . .?	How far is . . .?
Combien de temps . . .?	How long . . .?
Pouvez-vous . . .?	Can you . . .?
Pouvez-vous me dire . . .?	Can you tell me . . .?
Voulez-vous . . .?	Please will you . . .?
Voulez-vous me donner . . .?	Please will you give me . . .?
Je voudrais . . .	I would like . . .
Je cherche . . .	I am looking for . . .
Pouvez-vous m'aider, s'il vous plaît?	Can you help me, please?
Voulez-vous répéter cela, s'il vous plaît?	Would you repeat that, please?
Voulez-vous parler moins vite?	Please speak more slowly.
Je comprends.	I understand.
Je ne comprends pas.	I don't understand.
D'accord!	OK!
Est-ce qu'il y a . . .?	Is there . . .?
J'ai perdu . . .	I have lost . . .

Expressing your feelings

Attention!	Be careful!
C'est dommage.	What a pity.
Je préfère . . .	I prefer . . .
Je n'aime pas . . .	I don't like . . .
Je déteste . . .	I hate . . .
J'aime . . .	I like . . .
J'adore . . .	I love . . .
J'espère que . . .	I hope that . . .
Ça m'a plu.	I liked it.
Ça ne m'a pas plu.	I didn't like it.
Je suis déçu(e).	I am disappointed.
J'en suis content(e).	I am happy.
J'ai oublié.	I have forgotten.
Excusez-moi!	I am sorry!
Je regrette mais . . .	I am sorry but . . .
Au secours!	Help!
D'accord!	Agreed!
Je suis d'accord.	I agree.
Je ne suis pas d'accord.	I don't agree.
Félicitations!	Congratulations!
Santé!	Good health!
Bonne chance!	Good luck!
Bon voyage!	Have a good trip!
Bon appétit!	Enjoy your meal!
Je suis désolé(e).	I am very sorry.
Quelle surprise!	What a surprise!
Je vous (t')en prie.	Don't mention it.

J'en ai marre.	I am fed up.
Ne vous en faites pas. (Ne t'en fais pas.)	Don't worry.
Amusez-vous bien. (Amuses-toi bien.)	Have a good time.
Tant mieux!	So much the better!
Tant pis!	Too bad!
Bonne idée!	Good idea!
J'accepte.	I accept.
Je refuse.	I refuse.
Je crois que oui.	I think so.
Je ne pense pas.	I don't think so.
Ça m'est égal.	I don't mind.
Je m'ennuie.	I am bored.
J'ai peur.	I am frightened.

Public transport

VOCABULAIRE ESSENTIEL

BUYING TICKETS

first-class ticket	le billet de première classe
second-class ticket	le billet de deuxième classe
single ticket	aller simple (m)
return ticket	aller retour (m)
ticket-office	le guichet

FACILITIES

information office	le bureau de renseignements
left-luggage office	la consigne
lost property office	le bureau des objets trouvés
snack bar	le buffet
timetable	l'horaire (m)
waiting-room	la salle d'attente

TRAVELLING BY RAIL

carriage	la voiture
compartment	le compartiment
dining-car	le wagon-restaurant
platform	le quai
porter	le porteur
railway	le chemin de fer
sleeping-car	le wagon-lit
track	la voie

TRAVELLING BY AIR

air hostess	l'hôtesse de l'air
airport	l'aéroport
flight	le vol

TRAVELLING BY BUS, UNDERGROUND OR TAXI

bus	le car
bus station	la gare routière
bus stop	l'arrêt d'autobus
taxi rank	la station de taxis
underground	le métro
underground station	la station de métro

TRAVELLING BY SEA

hovercraft	l'aéroglisseur
ferry	le ferry
ship	le bateau

VERBS

to arrive	arriver
to book	réserver
to change (i.e. trains)	changer
to fly	voler
it is necessary	il faut
to land (planes)	atterrir
to leave	partir
to leave (e.g. luggage)	déposer
to miss (i.e. a train)	manquer
to stop	s'arrêter
to take off (i.e. planes)	décoller
to wait	attendre

OTHER WORDS			
		Have a good trip!	**Bon voyage!**
bag	**le sac**	late	**en retard**
by air	**en avion**	luggage	**les bagages** (m)
by train	**par le train**	passport	**le passeport**
direct	**direct**	seat	**la place**
door (of a vehicle)	**la portière**	suitcase	**la valise**
early	**en avance**	taken (i.e. a seat)	**occupé**
entrance	**l'entrée** (f)	traveller	**le voyageur**
exit	**la sortie**		

A toi de jouer

1 Ask for a second-class single to Paris.

2 Ask for a first-class return to Tours.

3 Say you want two tickets.

4 Find out if there is a bus/train to Bordeaux.

5 Find out what time it arrives/leaves.

6 Ask how often the trains to Paris are.

7 Say you would like to reserve a seat.

8 Say that you have a reserved ticket.

9 Find out where the station/the bus station/the underground station is.

10 Ask how long the journey takes.

11 Find out when the next flight is.

12 Ask where the ticket office is.

13 Ask where the information office is.

14 Find out where the left luggage/lost property office is.

15 Ask where the Paris train leaves from.

16 Find out which platform the Calais train leaves from.

17 Ask where the taxi rank/bus stop is.

18 Find out if there is a seat free in the carriage.

19 Say that the seat is taken.

20 Find out what time the plane takes off/lands.

21 Say that you would like to take a taxi.

22 Ask where you can find a taxi.

23 Find out if the train is direct.

24 Ask if it is necessary to change.

25 Ask where you must change.

26 Tell the driver to take you to a cheap hotel.

27 Ask for the snack bar.

28 Find out when the next/first/last bus leaves.

29 Say you want a non-smoking compartment.

30 Ask where you can put your luggage.

31 Ask if this is the right platform.

32 Ask where you should get off.

33 Find out if there is a dining-car/a sleeping-car.

34 Ask if there is a reduction/a supplement.

35 Find out where the toilets are.

36 Find out where the waiting-room is.

37 Ask if you can leave your luggage here.

38 Find out if the flight is late.

39 Ask if the train arrived early.

40 Say that you have lost your ticket.

41 Find out the price of a book of tickets.

42 Ask for a map of the underground.

43 Say you will arrive at 10 p.m.

44 Say you will set off at 2 a.m.

45 Ask your friend if he/she has anything to declare.

46 Say that you have just arrived.

47 Say that you will catch the ten o'clock train.

48 Tell your friend that you tried to phone from the station.

49 Tell your friend that you will phone from the airport.

50 Find out where you can find a porter.

Deux aller simple à Bordeaux, s'il vous plaît.

51 Ask the porter to help you with your luggage.

52 Say that you have missed your bus.

53 Find out if the bus goes to the town centre.

Pour les réponses, voir page 63

At the garage/ filling station

VOCABULAIRE ESSENTIEL

BREAKDOWNS

battery	**la batterie**
brakes	**les freins** (m)
breakdown	**la panne**
flat (tyre)	**crevé**
headlight	**le phare**
mechanic	**le mécanicien**
out of petrol	**la panne d'essence**
puncture	**la crevaison**
windscreen	**le pare-brise**

ROUTINE STOP

oil	**l'huile** (f)
petrol	**l'essence** (f)
petrol (four-star)	**le super**
petrol (lead-free)	**sans plomb**
pressure (of tyres)	**la pression**
road-map	**la carte routière**

toilets	**les toilettes** (f)
tyre	**le pneu**
water	**l'eau** (f)

ROADS

A-road	**la route nationale**
motorway	**l'autoroute** (f)

VERBS

to break down	**tomber en panne**
to check (i.e. the oil)	**vérifier**
to clean	**nettoyer**
to fill up (with petrol)	**faire le plein**
to park	**garer, stationner**
to repair	**réparer**
to work (i.e. the brakes)	**marcher**

A toi de jouer

1 Ask for 20 litres of high-grade petrol.

2 Ask for 10 litres of lead-free petrol.

3 Ask the attendant to fill up the tank.

4 Ask the attendant to check the oil.

5 Ask the attendant to check the tyres.

6 Ask the attendant to check the water.

7 Find out where the toilets are.

8 Ask if they sell road-maps.

9 Find out if you are on the right road for Paris.

10 Ask which way to go for Toulouse.

11 Find out if the road to Paris is an A-road or a motorway.

12 Find out where you can park.

13 Say your car has broken down.

14 Say you have left it two kilometres away.

15 Ask if he can help.

16 Ask if he can fix your car.

17 Ask if there is a mechanic available.

18 Say the brakes don't work.

19 Say you have a puncture.

20 Tell the attendant that a headlight is not working.

21 Say that the windscreen is broken.

22 Say you need a new battery.

23 Find out how much you owe.

24 Ask if you can phone from here.

25 Find out how far it is to Paris.

26 Find out where the nearest hotel is.

27 Ask if they sell sweets.

28 Ask the attendant to clean the windscreen.

29 Say you have run out of petrol.

30 Say you have had an accident.

31 Ask how long you will have to wait.

32 Ask how much it will cost.

Pour les réponses, voir page 65

Voulez-vous vérifier l'eau, s'il vous plaît?

At the customs

VOCABULAIRE ESSENTIEL

LUGGAGE
bag	**le sac**
luggage	**les bagages** (m)
suitcase	**la valise**

PROPERTY
passport	**le passeport**
present	**le cadeau**

perfume	**le parfum**
watch	**la montre**

OTHER WORDS
customs	**la douane**
customs officer	**le douanier**
to declare	**déclarer**

A toi de jouer

1 Say you are English/Irish/Scottish/Welsh.

2 Say you have nothing to declare.

3 Say you would like to declare a camera.

4 Tell the officer that you have two suitcases and a bag.

5 Say that the suitcase is yours.

6 Tell the officer that there are clothes and presents in your suitcase.

7 Say that you bought the watch in Switzerland two weeks ago.

8 Tell the officer that the perfume cost four hundred francs.

9 Ask if he/she wants to see your passport.

10 Tell the officer that you will be in France for two weeks.

11 Say that you are here on holiday.

Pour les réponses, voir page 67

At the campsite

EQUIPMENT

battery	**la pile**
camping equipment	**le matériel de camping**
caravan	**la caravane**
corkscrew	**le tire-bouchon**
gas bottle	**la bouteille de gaz**
tent	**la tente**
tin-opener	**l'ouvre-boîte** (m)

FACILITIES

drinking water	**l'eau potable** (f)
dustbin	**la poubelle**
electric socket	**la prise de courant**
pitch (for tent)	**l'emplacement** (m)
toilet block	**le bloc sanitaire**

OTHER WORDS

campsite	**le terrain de camping**

clean	**propre**
dirty	**sale**
extra payment	**le supplément**
match (for lighting a fire)	**l'allumette** (f)
shade	**l'ombre** (f)
warden	**le gardien**
washing (i.e. clothes)	**la lessive**
well-equipped	**bien équippé**
well-lit	**bien éclairé**

VERBS

to camp	**camper**
to do the washing-up	**faire la vaisselle**
to go camping	**faire du camping**
to need	**avoir besoin de**
to put up (a tent)	**monter (une tente)**
to stay	**rester**

A toi de jouer

1 Say you would like to reserve a pitch.

2 Ask if you can camp here.

3 Find out if they have space for a tent.

4 Say you have a tent/caravan.

5 Ask how much it is for a tent, two adults, four children and a car.

6 Say you would like to stay for two days.

7 Say you are alone.

8 Say that you will arrive the day after tomorrow.

9 Tell the warden that you will leave on Saturday.

10 Ask where your pitch is.

11 Say you would like a pitch in the shade.

12 Say you are English/Irish/Scottish/Welsh.

13 Ask if he/she wants to see your passport.

14 Find out when you must pay.

15 Say you would like to pay now.

16 Ask how you get to the campsite.

17 Find out if there are hot showers.

Vous avez perdu la clef de votre caravane? Utilisez un ouvre-boîte, monsieur.

18 Say you want a pitch near the toilet block.

19 Find out where the drinking water is.

20 Ask where you can wash clothes/dishes.

21 Ask about the regulations.

22 Say that your pitch is too near the dustbins.

23 Ask if you can borrow a tin-opener/corkscrew/some matches.

24 Ask if you can put up your tent over there.

25 Find out where the nearest electric socket is.

26 Ask how much it is per person.

27 Say it is too expensive.

28 Ask if there is a washing-machine on the site.

29 Ask if they serve hot meals.

30 Find out if there is a shop on the site.

31 Ask if you can light a fire.

32 Tell the warden that you are very pleased with the campsite.

33 Ask if the campsite has lots of facilities.

34 Say you need a gas bottle.

35 Say you need batteries.

36 Find out if the campsite is well-lit at night.

37 Ask if the campsite is closed at night.

38 Ask if you have to pay extra for that.

Pour les réponses, voir page 67

At the youth hostel

VOCABULAIRE ESSENTIEL

BEDDING

blanket	**la couverture**
sheet	**le drap**
sleeping-bag	**le sac de couchage**

PLACES

bathroom	**la salle de bains**
dining-room	**la salle à manger**
dormitory	**le dortoir**
games room	**la salle de jeux**
kitchen	**la cuisine**
shower	**la douche**
toilets	**les toilettes** (f), **le W.C.**

AT RECEPTION

all year	**toute l'année**
bed	**le lit**
card (membership)	**la carte**
closed	**fermé**
form (to fill in)	**la fiche**
full	**complet, complète**
open	**ouvert**

per day	**par jour**
per night	**par nuit**
per person	**par personne**
regulations	**les règlements**

OTHER WORDS

breakfast	**le petit déjeuner**
complaint	**la plainte**
dustbin	**la poubelle**
hot water	**l'eau chaude** (f)
meal	**le repas**
valuables	**les objets de valeur** (m)
youth hostel	**l'auberge de jeunesse** (f)

VERBS

to book	**réserver**
to cook	**faire de la cuisine**
to have dinner	**dîner**
to hire	**louer**
to pay	**payer**
to sleep	**dormir**

A toi de jouer

1 Say you have booked a bed.

2 Say you have not reserved a bed.

3 Ask if there is any room.

4 Ask if there are any free beds.

5 Say you will leave tomorrow/the day after tomorrow.

6 Say you will stay for three nights.

7 Tell the warden that there are two boys and two girls in your party.

8 Say you are English/Irish/Scottish/Welsh.

9 Find out how much it is per person per night.

10 Ask if there are shops nearby.

11 Find out if there are showers, a kitchen and a games room in the hostel.

12 Ask where the toilets/the dustbins are.

13 Tell the warden that you would like to pay now/later/tomorrow/on leaving.

14 Find out what time breakfast/lunch/dinner is served.

Puis-je louer un drap aussi, s'il vous plaît?

15 Ask what time the hostel closes.

16 Ask what time the office opens in the morning.

17 Ask what the regulations are.

18 Tell the warden that you have a sleeping-bag.

19 Say that you would like to hire a sleeping-bag/some sheets/some blankets.

20 Ask where the girls' and the boys' dormitories are.

21 Find out if alcohol is allowed.

22 Ask what time you must leave the hostel.

23 Find out if you have to fill in a form.

24 Enquire if there is hot water.

25 Ask what you must do before leaving.

26 Find out where you can leave valuables.

27 Say you have a complaint.

28 Ask the warden if he/she wants to see your card.

29 Find out if the hostel is full.

30 Ask if the hostel is open all year.

31 Enquire if you can cook in the hostel.

32 Ask if they serve meals.

33 Ask directions to the dining-room.

34 Ask where you can leave your bicycle.

35 Say you are sorry. You do not want a bed upstairs. Ask for a bed on the ground floor.

Pour les réponses, voir page 69

At the doctor's/at the scene of an accident

VOCABULAIRE ESSENTIEL

BUYING MEDICINE

antiseptic	l'antiseptique (m)
aspirin	l'aspirine (f)
bandage	le pansement
chemist's	la pharmacie
cotton wool	le coton hydrophile
cream (i.e. for sores)	la pommade
medicine	le médicament
plaster (for cuts)	le sparadrap
prescription	l'ordonnance (f)
receipt	le reçu
tablet	le comprimé

COMPLAINTS

flue	la grippe
having a cold	enrhumé
injured	blessé
seasickness	le mal de mer
sunburn	le coup de soleil
sunstroke	l'insolation (f)
temperature	la fièvre

SCENE OF AN ACCIDENT

ambulance	l'ambulance (f)
collision	la collision
doctor	le médecin
driving licence	le permis de conduire
fault	la faute
fire	l'incendie (f)
firemen	les pompiers (m)
insurance	l'assurance (f)
serious	grave

OTHER WORDS

better	mieux
dentist	le dentiste
stomach	le ventre
throat	la gorge
tooth	la dent

VERBS

to brake	freiner
to break	casser
to burn	brûler
to cough	tousser
to cut oneself	se couper
to fall	tomber
to feel	se sentir
to hurt oneself	se faire mal
to knock over	renverser
to stay in bed	garder le lit
to sting	piquer
to vomit	vomir

A toi de jouer

1 Ask if he/she can help you.

2 Ask him/her to phone a doctor.

3 Ask him/her to phone for an ambulance.

4 Say you need a dentist.

5 Say you would like to see the doctor.

6 Say you have had an accident.

7 Say you have toothache.

8 Say you have a sore throat.

9 Say you have a headache.

10 Say you have a pain in your stomach.

11 Say you have broken your arm/leg.

12 Say he has broken his arm/leg.

13 Say you have a cold.

14 Say you have burnt yourself.

15 Say you have burnt your arm.

16 Say he has sunstroke/sunburn.

17 Say she has flu.

18 Say you have cut yourself.

19 Say you have cut your leg.

20 Say that you fell.

21 Say that you had a car accident.

22 Say that you have a temperature.

23 Say that you are seasick.

24 Say that you have been stung.

25 Say that you have a cough.

26 Say that you have been sick three times.

27 Say that your friend is injured.

28 Ask if you must come back to see the doctor again.

29 Find out if you have to stay in bed.

30 Find out if you need a prescription.

31 Find out where the chemist's is.

32 Ask for a receipt.

33 Find out how long you must take the tablets for.

34 Say you would like to buy some cotton wool, a bandage, some plasters and some antiseptic.

35 Say that your sister feels ill.

36 Ask for some aspirin.

37 When asked how long you have been ill, say for two hours/ since yesterday.

38 Ask how often you should take the tablets.

39 Say that you feel ill/better.

40 Find out if he has anything for a sore throat.

41 Say that you are taking no medicines.

42 Say that you have insurance.

43 Ask him/her to phone the police/fire brigade.

44 Say that the accident was serious.

45 Say it was not your fault; say it was the fault of the other driver.

46 Find out if they sell a cream for sunburn.

47 Say that your father braked but there was a collision.

48 Say there was a fire in the engine.

49 Say that your father's driving licence is at the hotel.

50 Say that a cyclist knocked over an old man who was crossing the street.

51 Say that it hurts.

Pour les réponses, voir page 71

Voulez-vous téléphoner pour une ambulance?

Shopping for food and drink

VOCABULAIRE ESSENTIEL

SHOPS

baker's	**la boulangerie**
butcher's	**la boucherie**
cake shop	**la pâtisserie**
chemist's	**la pharmacie**
department store	**le grand magasin**
fishmonger's	**la poissonerie**
food store	**l'alimentation** (f)
greengrocer's	**le marchand de fruits**
grocer's	**l'épicerie**
market	**le marché**
pork butcher's	**la charcuterie**
supermarket	**le supermarché**
tobacconist's	**le bureau de tabac**

FRUIT

apple	**la pomme**
apricot	**l'abricot** (m)
banana	**la banane**
cherry	**la cerise**
fruit	**le fruit**
grape	**le raisin**
melon	**le melon**
orange	**l'orange** (f)
peach	**la pêche**
pear	**la poire**
pineapple	**l'ananas** (m)
strawberry	**la fraise**

VEGETABLES

cabbage	**le chou**
carrot	**la carotte**
cauliflower	**le chou-fleur**
lettuce	**la laitue**
mushroom	**le champignon**
onion	**l'oignon** (m)
peas	**les petits pois** (m)
potato	**la pomme de terre**
runner bean	**le haricot vert**
vegetable	**le légume**

MEAT

beef	**le boeuf**
chicken	**le poulet**
ham	**le jambon**
lamb	**l'agneau** (m)
meat	**la viande**
mutton	**le mouton**
rabbit	**le lapin**
sausage (continental style)	**le saucisson**
sausage (British style)	**la saucisse**
steak	**le bifteck**

DESSERT		mineral water	l'eau minérale (f)
cake	le gâteau	tea	le thé
cheese	le fromage	wine	le vin
dessert	le dessert		
ice-cream	la glace	**OTHER WORDS**	
DRINK		egg	l'oeuf (m)
beer	la bière	pâté	le pâté
coffee	le café	pepper	le poivre
drink	la boisson	salt	le sel
fruit juice	le jus de fruit	seafood	les fruits de mer (m)
milk	le lait	slice	la tranche

A toi de jouer

1 Say you would like a loaf of bread.

2 Ask how much it is.

3 Say you would like to buy some cakes.

4 Ask for five hundred grammes of ham.

5 Say you would like some beef/mutton/rabbit.

6 Ask for two hundred and fifty grammes of sausage.

7 Find out if there is a grocer's shop open in the area.

8 Say you would like to buy some cigarettes for your father.

9 Ask for two hundred grammes of cherries/bananas/
oranges/peaches/pears/apples/strawberries/
apricots/grapes.

10 Ask for a pineapple/a melon.

11 Find out where you can buy vegetables.

12 Ask for a pound of runner beans/onions/peas/
potatoes/mushrooms/cabbage/carrots/cauliflower.

13 Ask for a lettuce.

14 Find out if there is a butcher's shop nearby.

15 Ask for a kilogramme of chicken/rabbit/steak.

16 Ask if the meat is good in that shop.

17 Find out where you can buy seafood.

18 Ask for a pound of sausage/pâté.

19 Buy two litres of red wine and one litre of white wine.

20 Ask for five litres of beer.

21 Ask for a jar of coffee.

22 Ask for a bottle of mineral water.

23 Say you would like some fruit juice.

24 Ask for two litres of milk.

25 Ask for a packet of tea.

26 Ask for a dozen eggs.

27 Find out where you can
buy salt/pepper.

J'ai acheté ce fromage ici et il n'est pas bon.

28 Ask for a slice of cheese.

29 Say you are buying food for a picnic.

30 Ask for two hundred grammes of butter.

31 Find out if they sell sweets/chocolate.

32 Ask for a packet of sugar.

33 Say you do not like it and that you are not going to buy it.

34 Say it is too dear.

35 Say he/she has given you too much/little.

36 Say you will take it.

37 Say you want nothing else.

38 Find out how much you owe.

39 Ask for change.

40 Say you bought this cheese here. Say it is not nice. Ask for your money back.

41 Say you only have a hundred-franc note.

42 Ask if you can choose the fruit that you want.

43 Ask for something a little larger.

44 Ask if he/she has anything cheaper.

45 Find out where the cash desk is.

46 Ask for a box/plastic bag.

47 Find out if you can pay with a cheque or credit card.

48 Ask if they are open on Sunday.

49 Find out what time they open/close.

Pour les réponses, voir page 73

Shopping for clothes and toiletries

MATERIALS

cotton	**le coton**
leather	**le cuir**
nylon	**le nylon**
wool	**la laine**

SIZE OF CLOTHING

big	**grand**
long	**long(ue)**
short	**court**
size	**la taille**
size (of shoes)	**la pointure**
small	**petit**
tight	**étroit**
too	**trop**
wide	**large**

BAD-WEATHER CLOTHES

anorak	**l'anorak** (m)
coat	**le manteau**
glove	**le gant**
hat	**le chapeau**
jumper	**le tricot**
pullover	**le pull(over)**
raincoat	**l'imperméable** (m)
scarf	**le foulard/ l'écharpe** (f)

GOOD-WEATHER CLOTHES

shorts	**le short**

swimming- costume	**le maillot de bain**
T-shirt	**le tee-shirt**

ON YOUR FEET

boot	**la botte**
shoe	**la chaussure**
slipper	**la pantoufle**
sock	**la chaussette**

OTHER CLOTHES

blouse	**le chemisier**
dress	**la robe**
dressing-gown	**la robe de chambre**
jacket	**le blouson/la veste**
jeans	**le jean**
pyjamas	**le pyjama**
shirt	**la chemise**
skirt	**la jupe**
suit	**le costume**
tie	**la cravate**
tights	**les collants** (m)
trousers	**le pantalon**

TOILETRIES

comb	**le peigne**
shampoo	**le shampooing**
soap	**le savon**
toothbrush	**la brosse à dents**
toothpaste	**le dentifrice**

OTHER WORDS		VERBS	
changing cubicle	**la cabine d'essayage**	to put on	**mettre**
clothes	**les vêtements** (m)	to try on	**essayer**
handkerchief	**le mouchoir**	to window-shop	**faire du lèche-**
pair	**la paire**		**vitrines**

A toi de jouer

1 Ask what size it is.

2 Ask what size the shoes are.

3 Ask if the shirt is cotton/nylon.

4 Ask if the pullover is made of wool.

5 Say you would like to buy some slippers.

6 Find out if the gloves are made of leather.

7 Say that you like this jacket.

8 Find out where the changing rooms are.

9 Say you would like to try on this pair of trousers.

10 Find out if they have the same skirt in blue.

11 Say the dress is too long/short/tight/wide/big/small.

12 Ask the assistant to gift-wrap the scarf.

13 Find out on which floor the men's department is.

14 Ask for the cash desk.

15 Find out where the lift/exit is.

16 Find out what time they open/close.

17 Ask if you can listen to this record.

18 Request a plastic bag.

19 Ask if you can exchange the coat.

20 Say that it is the wrong size.

21 Find out if there is another shop which sells jumpers.

22 Tell him/her that he/she has made a mistake.

23 Ask your friend what he/she is going to buy.

24 Ask if this T-shirt suits you.

25 Find out where you can buy soap/shampoo/a comb/a toothbrush/toothpaste.

26 Say you would like to window-shop.

27 Say it is too expensive.

28 Say it is very cheap.

29 Ask for your size.

30 Find out if they have anything cheaper.

31 Find out where you should pay.

Pour les réponses, voir page 75

At the cleaner's/launderette

VOCABULAIRE ESSENTIEL

change (for washing-machine)	la monnaie	to clean	nettoyer
		to dry-clean	nettoyer à sec
		to mend (clothes)	raccommoder (les vêtements)
cleaner's	la teinturerie		
coin	la pièce	washing-machine	la machine à laver
launderette	la laverie automatique	washing-powder	la lessive/le détergent

A toi de jouer

1 Ask if your trousers can be cleaned.

2 Ask if your blouse can be mended.

3 Find out how long it will take.

4 Say you would like to wash these clothes.

5 Ask for change for the washing-machine.

6 Find out which coins are needed for the washing-machine.

7 Ask where you can buy washing-powder.

Pour les réponses, voir page 77

At the café/restaurant

VOCABULAIRE ESSENTIEL

ON THE TABLE

cup	la tasse
fork	la fourchette
glass	le verre
knife	le couteau
mustard	la moutarde
pepper	le poivre
plate	l'assiette (f)
salt	le sel
saucer	la soucoupe
spoon	la cuillère
tablecloth	la nappe
vinegar	le vinaigre

FACILITIES

area outside a café	la terrasse
in the shade	à l'ombre
in the sun	au soleil
telephone	le téléphone
toilets	les toilettes (f)

ORDERING

dessert	le dessert
eighty-franc menu	le menu à quatre-vingts francs
first course	l'entrée (f)
menu	le menu/la carte
starter	le hors-d'oeuvre
today's special	le plat du jour
waiter	le garçon
waitress	la serveuse

STEAKS

medium	à point
rare	saignant
well-done	bien cuit

FOOD

breakfast	le petit déjeuner
chips	les frites (f)
cucumber	le concombre
ice-cream (vanilla, strawberry, chocolate)	la glace (à la vanille, à la fraise, au chocolat)
mussels	les moules (f)
oysters	les huîtres (f)
pork chop	la côte de porc
rice	le riz
salad	la salade
sandwich (cheese, ham, pâté)	le sandwich (au fromage, au jambon, au pâté)
sardine	la sardine
soup	le potage/la soupe
trout	la truite

See also pages 24-5 in the 'Shopping for food' section.

PAYING THE BILL

bill	l'addition (f)
owner	le patron
included	compris
mistake	l'erreur (f)
service	le service
tip	le pourboire

OTHER WORDS		VERBS	
Cheers!	**Santé!**	to be hungry	**avoir faim**
choice	**le choix**	to be thirsty	**avoir soif**
delicious	**délicieux**	to book	**réserver**
Enjoy your meal!	**Bon appétit!**	to choose	**choisir**
ill	**malade**	to clean	**nettoyer**
tray	**le plateau**	to order	**commander**

A toi de jouer

1 Call the waiter/waitress and ask for the menu.

2 Say you would like to leave a tip.

3 Say you would like to reserve a table.

4 Say you have reserved a table.

5 Ask the waiter for a cup/saucer/knife/fork/spoon/glass.

6 Say that the tablecloth is dirty.

7 Tell the waiter that you would like to order.

8 Ask the waiter to remove the tray.

9 Ask for the bill.

10 Say 'Cheers!' and 'Enjoy your meal'.

11 Ask the waiter to choose a wine.

12 Find out where the telephone is/the toilets are.

13 Find out if service is included.

14 Say that you are hungry/thirsty.

15 Say that you want your steak rare/medium/well-done.

16 Say that the meal is delicious.

17 Ask what he/she would like for dessert.

18 Say that you feel ill.

19 Ask for the eighty-franc menu.

20 Ask for today's special.

21 Ask for pork chop with onions, peas and chips.

22 Find out if they serve breakfast.

23 Say you would like black/white coffee.

24 Order soup, rabbit, rice/potatoes.

25 Say you would like a cheese/pâté/ham sandwich.

26 Order oysters/mussels.

27 Order trout/sardines.

28 Say you would like some cucumber in the salad.

A quelle heure servez-vous le petit déjeuner?

29 Ask for cherries/a banana/a melon/an orange/a peach/a pear/an apple/some strawberries/some apricots/some pineapple/some grapes.

30 Order chicken, runner beans, mushrooms and carrots.

31 Say you do not like cabbage.

32 Tell the waiter that the cauliflower is not nice.

33 Find out if you can have lamb.

34 Find out what drinks they serve.

35 Ask for a litre of white/red wine.

36 Order a beer.

37 Say you would like some fruit juice/mineral water/milk/tea.

38 Say you would like a boiled/fried/poached/scrambled egg.

39 Ask for salt/pepper/vinegar/mustard.

40 Ask for a slice of ham.

41 Ask the waiter to clean the table.

42 Say you would like to be outside in the sun/shade.

43 Ask for a table for two near the window.

44 Tell the waiter that he has made a mistake.

45 Say you do not understand the menu. Ask what this dish is.

46 Ask him/her to close/open the window.

47 Ask for more.

48 Ask for an ashtray.

49 Tell the waiter he has forgotten the vanilla ice-cream.

50 Ask for change for the telephone.

51 Say the food is cold.

52 Say that your fork is dirty.

53 Say that you want something cool/hot to drink.

54 Say that you are too hot/cold.

55 Say that you only had a lemonade and an orange juice.

56 Ask him to check the bill.

57 Say you are in a hurry. Find out how long it's going to take.

58 Say that there are four of you.

59 Explain to your friend that this dish is fish, not meat.

60 Find out if they accept credit cards.

61 Say you did not order any wine.

62 Find out if there is a choice of vegetables.

63 Say that it smells good.

64 Ask your friend if he/she has decided.

65 Say that it is too expensive.

66 Find out which wine he/she would like.

Pour les réponses, voir page 77

At the post office

V O C A B U L A I R E   E S S E N T I E L

ITEMS TO SEND

letter	**la lettre**
packet	**le paquet**
parcel	**le colis**
postal order	**le mandat**
postcard	**la carte postale**
telegram	**le télégramme**

FACILITIES

counter	**le guichet**
phone booth	**la cabine téléphonique**
post-box	**la boîte aux lettres**
poste restante	**la poste restante**

SENDING THINGS OFF

abroad	**à l'étranger** (m)
address	**l'adresse** (f)

by air	**par avion**
two-franc stamp	**le timbre à deux francs**
United Kingdom	**le Royaume Uni**

OTHER WORDS

coin	**la pièce**
collection (of mail)	**la levée**
fragile	**fragile**
mail	**le courrier**

VERBS

to fill in a form	**remplir un formulaire**
to post	**poster**
to send	**envoyer**

A toi de jouer

1 Ask where the post office is.

2 Ask if there is a post-box in the post office.

3 Find out how much it costs to send a letter/postcard to England.

4 Say you would like to send a letter to Great Britain.

5 Say you would like to send a parcel.

6 Find out if a packet has arrived for you.

7 Say you would like two five-franc stamps.

8 Find out what time they open/close.

9 Ask if there is a letter for you at the poste restante counter.

10 Find out if there is a phone booth here.

11 Say you need coins for a phone call to the United Kingdom.

12 Say that you want to send a telegram.

13 Ask how much it is to send a telegram.

14 Find out how long it takes for a letter to reach the United Kingdom.

15 Ask if there is a special post-box for letters going abroad.

16 Find out where you can post a letter.

17 Say you would like to phone England.

18 Say you would like to buy a postal order.

Vous voulez 100,000 francs? Il faut remplir un formulaire, monsieur.

19 Find out which counter you need.

20 Say you want to send the letter by airmail.

21 Find out if you have to fill in a form.

22 Ask if the post office is open on Saturdays.

23 Find out if there is a faster service.

24 Ask when the next collection is.

Pour les réponses, voir page 80

On the telephone

VOCABULAIRE ESSENTIEL			
dialling tone	**la tonalité**	phone number	**le numéro de téléphone**
directory	**l'annuaire** (m)		
Hello	**Allô**	reverse-charge call	**le PCV**
operator	**l'opératrice** (f)		
phone call	**le coup de téléphone**	to dial	**marquer**

A toi de jouer

1 Find out where the nearest telephone is.

2 Ask for the telephone directory.

3 Ask if you can speak to Jean.

4 Say you can't hear the dialling tone.

5 Ask for the number of the tourist office.

6 Say you would like to speak to the operator.

7 Say you want to make a reverse-charge call.

8 When you have picked up the phone, say 'Hello!' and say 'It is Melanie speaking'.

9 Ask the caller if he/she wants to leave a message.

10 Say you cannot hear. Ask the caller to speak more slowly.

11 Ask the person not to hang up.

12 Say you have got the wrong number.

Pour les réponses, voir page 81

Opératrice. Je veux téléphoner à Mars, s'il vous plaît.

At the bank/ exchange office

VOCABULAIRE ESSENTIEL

MONEY

currency	**la monnaie**
pound sterling	**la livre sterling**
ten-franc note	**le billet de dix francs**

commission	**la commission**
counter	**le guichet**
per cent	**pour cent**
rate of exchange	**le cours du change**

ITEMS TO TAKE

banker's card	**la carte bancaire**
credit card	**la carte de crédit**
passport	**le passeport**
traveller's cheque	**le chèque de voyage**

VERBS

to be worth	**valoir**
to change	**changer**
to go to the cash desk	**passer à la caisse**
to queue	**faire la queue**
to sign	**signer**

OTHER WORDS

cashier's desk	**la caisse**

A toi de jouer

1 Find out where you must queue.

2 Say you want to change some pounds into francs.

3 Say you want to change some traveller's cheques into francs.

4 Find out at which counter.

5 Ask if it is your turn.

6 Ask what the rate of exchange is.

7 Ask if he/she wants to see your passport.

8 Say you have forgotten your passport.

9 Say you will go and get your passport.

10 Find out where you have to sign.

11 Find out how much the pound is worth.

12 Ask if you must go to the cashier's desk.

13 Say you have a credit card.

14 Say you have a banker's card.

15 Find out if you have to pay a commission.

16 Ask if the commission is ten per cent.

17 Say you would like hundred-franc notes.

18 Say you would like some ten-franc coins.

19 Tell the clerk that all your money has been stolen.

20 Ask him/her to phone your bank in England.

21 Tell him/her to ask your bank to send some money.

Pour les réponses, voir page 82

At the police station/ lost property office

VOCABULAIRE ESSENTIEL

PROPERTY

camera	**l'appareil-photo** (m)
cheque-book	**le carnet de chèques**
handbag	**le sac à main**
passport	**le passeport**
purse	**le porte-monnaie**
ring	**la bague**
suitcase	**la valise**
wallet	**le porte-feuille**
watch	**la montre**

VILLAINS

burglar	**le cambrioleur**
thief	**le voleur**

OTHER WORDS

colour	**la couleur**
description	**la description**
form (to fill in)	**la fiche**

gold	**l'or** (m)
lost property office	**le bureau des objets trouvés**
make (e.g. of camera)	**la marque**
police station	**le commisariat de police**
reward	**la récompense**

VERBS

to borrow	**emprunter**
to burgle	**cambrioler**
to contain	**contenir**
to describe	**décrire**
to leave (behind)	**laisser**
to lend	**prêter**
to lose	**perdre**
to run away	**se sauver**
to steal	**voler**

A toi de jouer

1 Say that you have lost something. Find out where the police station is.

2 Say that you have found something. Find out where the lost property office is.

3 Say the camera is quite large.

4 Say that you do not know the make.

5 Say that you bought it two years ago.

6 Say that it is five years old.

7 Tell the policeman that it is worth £100.

8 Say that the suitcase contained clothes, a watch and a gold ring.

9 Say that the purse contained twenty pounds.

10 Say that the wallet contained a thousand francs.

11 Say that you did not see the thief/burglar.

BUREAU DES OBJETS TROUVÉS

Vous avez perdu votre femme? Oui, elle est ici . . .

12 Say that you lost it in front of the ticket-office.

13 Say that you left it in your room.

14 Say that the suitcase was in your father's car.

15 Say that you lost it two hours ago/yesterday/the day before yesterday.

16 Ask if the ring has been found.

17 Say that you are a British tourist.

18 Say that the handbag is your sister's.

19 Say that the camera is yours.

20 Ask if you must pay.

21 Ask what you must do now.

22 Say that you will return tomorrow.

23 Say that you will write.

24 Say that you will phone.

25 Say that your car has been stolen.

26 Say that a lot of things have been stolen from your car.

27 Say that you have lost your traveller's cheques/passport.

28 Ask if you can borrow some money.

29 Ask if he/she wants to lend you some money.

30 Say that the thief ran away.

31 Say it was a present from your aunt.

32 Say that you are very angry/disappointed/surprised/ pleased.

Pour les réponses, voir page 83

At the tourist information office

VOCABULAIRE ESSENTIEL

PLACES TO GO

amusements	**les distractions** (f)
circus	**le cirque**
concert	**le concert**
disco	**la disco**
museum	**le musée**
place of interest	**le lieu d'intérêt**
show	**le spectacle**
theatre	**le théâtre**
trip	**l'excursion** (f)
zoo	**le jardin zoologique**

INFORMATION

brochure	**la brochure, le dépliant**
information	**les renseignements** (m)
map of the area	**la carte de la région**

timetable	**l'horaire** (m)
town plan	**le plan de la ville**

OTHER WORDS

information office	**le bureau de renseignements**
seat	**la place**
ticket	**le billet**
tourist office	**le syndicat d'initiative**

VERBS

to be interested in	**s'intéresser à**
to book	**réserver**
to go for walks	**faire des promenades** (f)
to hire	**louer**
to visit	**visiter**

A toi de jouer

1 Say you are a British tourist.

2 Ask if he/she can give you information on the area.

3 Find out if he/she has any brochures.

4 Ask for a map of the town.

5 Ask for a map of the area.

6 Ask for a bus timetable.

7 Ask for a list of hotels and campsites.

8 Find out what the places of interest are.

9 Ask for information about the castle.

10 Say you would like information about the museum.

11 Find out if there are any trips.

12 Ask what there is to do in the evenings.

13 Find out if there are any shows/amusements.

14 Find out what time the museum opens/closes.

15 Say you like sports. Find out if there are any facilities.

16 Ask if you can hire skis/a bicycle.

17 Ask if you can buy tickets here.

Vous voulez visiter le château ce soir? Très bien, mademoiselle.

18 Find out if there is a circus/theatre/concert in the area.

19 Say you are interested in castles.

Pour les réponses, voir page 84

Asking the way

VOCABULAIRE ESSENTIEL

DIRECTIONS		before	**avant**
straight on	**tout droit**	behind	**derrière**
to (on) the left	**à gauche**	beside	**à côté de**
to (on) the right	**à droite**	five kilometres away	**à cinq kilomètres**
		five minutes away	**à cinq minutes**
HOW TO GET THERE		opposite	**en face de**
by bus	**en autobus**		
by taxi	**en taxi**	**OTHER WORDS**	
by train	**par le train**	area	**la région**
by underground	**en métro**	first	**premier (ière)**
on foot	**à pied**	map (of town)	**le plan**
		motorway	**l'autoroute** (f)
LANDMARKS		road-map	**la carte routière**
bridge	**le pont**	second	**deuxième**
bus stop	**l'arrêt d'autobus** (m)		
corner	**le coin**	**VERBS**	
crossroads	**le carrefour**	to carry on	**continuer**
roundabout	**le rond-point**	to cross	**traverser**
town centre	**le centre-ville**	to follow	**suivre**
traffic lights	**le feu rouge**	to get lost	**se perdre**
		to go down	**descendre**
POSITION		to go up	**monter**
after	**après**	to turn	**tourner**
at the end of	**au bout de**		

A toi de jouer

1 Say 'Excuse me' to a passer-by.

2 Say that you are lost.

3 Ask for directions to the town centre.

4 Ask if it is far.

5 Ask how far it is.

6 Tell him/her to turn right at the crossroads.

7 Tell him/her to turn left after the bank.

8 Tell him/her to cross the bridge and go straight on.

9 Tell him/her to go up the road to the supermarket.

10 Tell him/her to go down the road as far as the traffic lights.

11 Say it is opposite the cinema.

12 Tell him/her to follow the road as far as the roundabout.

13 Say the bus stop is on the left.

14 Tell him/her to take the first road on the right.

15 Tell him/her to take the second road after the bus stop.

16 Tell him/her to go straight on as far as the corner of the street.

17 Find out if he/she has a road-map/map of the town.

18 Tell him/her to take the motorway.

19 Say that you do not know the area.

20 Tell him/her that it is five kilometres away.

21 Say it is five minutes' walk away.

22 Tell him/her to take a taxi/tube/bus.

23 Tell him/her that it is behind the baker's.

24 Find out what number bus you must take.

25 Say that you will go with him/her.

26 Tell him/her to go down the corridor and take the lift to the first floor.

27 Say you do not understand.

28 Ask him/her to repeat that.

29 Ask where you can find a taxi.

Pour les réponses, voir page 85

Pour aller à Mars? Continuez tout droit jusqu'à la lune. Tournez à droite, continuez deux ans et vous êtes arrivés!

At the cinema

VOCABULAIRE ESSENTIEL

TYPES OF FILM

adventure film	le film d'aventure
comedy film	le film comique
detective film	le film policier
horror film	le film d'épouvante
romantic film	le film d'amour
science-fiction film	le film de science-fiction
spy film	le film d'espionnage
war film	le film de guerre
western	le western

DETAILS OF FILM

English version	la version anglaise

performance	la séance
star	la vedette
subtitle	le sous-titre

GETTING TO YOUR SEAT

seat	la place
tip	le pourboire
usherette	l'ouvreuse (f)

OTHER WORDS

circle	le balcon
interval	l'entracte (m)
stalls	l'orchestre (m)
to book	réserver

A toi de jouer

1 Ask your friend what film is showing at the cinema.

2 Find out if the film has subtitles.

3 Find out if the film is in French.

4 Say you would like to book two seats.

5 Ask your friend if he/she would like to go to the cinema this evening.

6 Ask your friend if you must give a tip to the usherette.

7 Find out what time the film starts.

8 Find out what time the film finishes.

9 Find out if there is an interval.

10 Ask how much a seat in the circle costs.

11 Say you would like a seat in the stalls.

12 Say that you liked the film.

13 Say that you did not like the film.

14 Find out if there is a reduction for groups.

15 Say that you prefer detective films.

16 Suggest that you meet in front of the cinema.

17 Ask what sort of film it is.

18 When your friend says it was a bad film, say that you do not agree.

19 Ask your friend if he/she liked the film.

20 When your friend says the film was good, say you agree.

Pour les réponses, voir page 86

Tu viens au cinéma? On joue un film de science-fiction!

At the hotel

VOCABULAIRE ESSENTIEL

TYPES OF ROOM

double room	**la chambre pour deux personnes**
family room	**la chambre de famille**
room with double bed	**la chambre avec un lit double**
room with two single beds	**la chambre avec deux lits**
room with single bed	**la chambre avec un lit**
single room	**la chambre pour une personne**

PLACES

bathroom	**la salle de bains**
car-park	**le parking**
corridor	**le couloir**
floor (i.e. storey)	**l'étage** (m)
ground floor	**au premier étage**
lift	**l'ascenseur** (m)
shower	**la douche**
toilet	**le W.C.**

CHECKING IN AND OUT

bed	**le lit**
bill	**la note**
cheque	**le chèque**
credit card	**la carte de crédit**
free (i.e. not occupied)	**libre**
full	**complet**

full board and lodging	**la pension complète**
half board	**la demi-pension**
included	**compris**
luggage	**les bagages** (m)
not included	**non compris**
number	**le numéro**
suitcase	**la valise**

ITEMS YOU MIGHT NEED

blanket	**la couverture**
coat-hanger	**le cintre**
key	**la clé/clef**
pillow	**l'oreiller** (m)
soap	**le savon**
toilet-paper	**le papier hygiénique**
towel	**la serviette**

COMPLAINTS

blocked	**bouché(e)**
leak	**la fuite**
noise	**le bruit**
tap	**le robinet**
too much	**trop**

VERBS

to book	**réserver**
to fill in a form	**remplir une fiche**
to park	**garer, stationner**
to work (i.e. to function)	**marcher**

A toi de jouer

1 Say you would like to book a room.

2 Say that you have booked a room.

3 Say that you would like a single room.

4 Say that you would like a double room.

5 Say that you would like a room with a single bed.

6 Say that you would like a room with a double bed.

7 Say that you would like a room with twin beds.

8 Say that you would like a family room.

9 Ask if they have a room with a shower or a bathroom.

10 Say that you will stay for four nights.

11 Say that you would like to leave tomorrow morning.

12 Tell the receptionist that you would like to leave very early.

13 Say that you want a room on the ground floor.

14 Ask what floor your room is on.

15 Find out the number of your room.

16 Find out if they serve meals.

17 Ask what time breakfast is served.

18 Ask if breakfast is included.

19 Ask if they have a room free.

20 Say you are English/Irish/Scottish/Welsh.

21 Find out if you have to fill in a form.

22 Ask for your key.

23 Ask for your bill.

24 Say the bill is not correct.

25 Tell the receptionist that you would like to pay by cheque or credit card.

26 Find out if there is a cinema nearby.

27 Ask for directions to the dining-room.

28 Say that there is no soap in your room.

29 Say that you would like an extra pillow.

30 Say that you are not happy with your room. Ask them to phone another hotel.

31 Say you would like to complain.

32 Say that there is no towel in your room.

33 Say that you have lost your key.

34 Find out if they have anything cheaper.

35 Ask if you can take up your luggage now.

36 Find out if there is a car-park nearby.

37 Say you want a room which overlooks the beach.

38 Say you will take these rooms.

39 Tell the receptionist that you have reserved a room by telephone.

40 Tell the receptionist that the lift doesn't work.

41 Say you would like more coat-hangers.

42 Say that the tap is leaking.

43 Say that the light is not working.

44 Say that the wash-basin is blocked.

45 Say that your room is too noisy.

46 Tell the receptionist that you want a different room.

47 Say that you are very disappointed.

48 Ask the receptionist for another blanket.

Pour les réponses, voir page 87

Visiting and receiving an exchange partner

VOCABULAIRE ESSENTIEL

ON ARRIVAL

clothes	les vêtements (m)
pleased to meet you	enchanté(e)
present (i.e. gift)	le cadeau
suitcase	la valise
tired	fatigué(e)
tiring	fatigant
welcome	la bienvenue

IN THE BATHROOM

bath	le bain
shower	la douche
soap	le savon
toothpaste	le dentifrice
towel	la serviette

DESCRIBING YOURSELF OVER THE PHONE

curly (hair)	frisé
fat	gros (grosse)
glasses	les lunettes (f)
long (hair)	long
quite	assez
short (hair)	court
small	petit
straight (hair)	raide
tall	haut
thin	mince

OTHER WORDS

downstairs	en bas
party (young people's)	la boum
upstairs	en haut

VERBS

to borrow	emprunter
to clear the table	débarrasser la table
to do the washing-up	faire la vaisselle
to get to know	connaître
to go to bed	se coucher
to help	aider
to hurt oneself	se faire mal
to introduce	présenter
to lay the table	mettre la table
to rest	se reposer
to share	partager
to show	faire voir

A toi de jouer

1 Say that you are pleased to meet him/her.

2 Say that he/she is welcome.

3 Introduce him/her to your brother.

4 Say that it is a present from your parents.

5 Say that you have a brother and two sisters.

6 Find out where your room/the bathroom is.

7 Say you will show him/her to his/her room.

8 Tell him/her that the bathroom is upstairs, on the left.

9 Say that you would like to phone your parents.

10 Ask if he/she would like to phone his/her parents.

11 Find out what time breakfast is.

12 Tell your partner that breakfast is at eight o'clock.

13 Say you are tired and that you would like to go to bed.

14 Ask if he/she is tired.

15 Find out if he/she wants to go to bed.

16 Say that the journey was very tiring.

17 Say that you like French food.

18 Ask if he/she likes English food.

19 Say that you do not like cabbage.

20 Ask if there is any food that he/she does not like.

21 Find out what time you leave tomorrow.

22 Ask where you can put your clothes.

23 Ask where you can put your suitcase.

24 Ask where you can meet.

25 Say you would like to meet his/her friends.

26 Ask if he/she would like to meet your friends.

27 Ask if there is anything that he/she would like to do.

28 Find out what he/she wants to do.

29 Say you would like to go out.

30 Say that you would like to go to the beach.

31 Suggest that you meet outside the station.

32 You are phoning your exchange partner. Say that you are tall/small.

33 Say that you wear glasses.

Je ne veux pas partager ma chambre!

34 Say that your hair is short/long.

35 Say that your hair is curly/straight.

36 Say that your hair is brown/black/fair.

37 Say that you will be wearing a green coat and jeans.

38 Say that you feel ill.

39 Say that you have hurt yourself.

40 Ask what he/she will be wearing.

41 Ask if he/she is ill.

42 Find out if he/she has hurt himself/herself.

43 Find out where you can wash your dirty clothes.

44 Ask if he/she has any dirty clothes.

45 Ask if you can watch the television.

46 Ask him/her if he/she wants to watch the television.

47 Say you would like to help his/her mother.

48 Say you will lay/clear the table.

49 Offer to wash the dishes.

50 Say that you would like to go to the party.

51 Ask if he/she wants to go to the party.

52 Find out how you will get back from the town.

53 Say that you can come back by bus.

54 Say that you do not want to share a room.

55 Ask if he/she has soap/a towel/toothpaste.

56 Say that you need soap/a towel/toothpaste.

57 Ask if he/she would like a bath/a shower.

58 Say that you would like to have a bath/shower.

59 Say that you are hungry/thirsty/hot/cold.

60 Say you would like to rest.

61 Say you would like to borrow some money.

Pour les réponses, voir page 90

Les réponses

Public transport

1 Je voudrais un aller simple de deuxième classe à Paris.

2 Je voudrais un aller retour de première classe à Tours.

3 Je voudrais deux billets.

4 Est-ce qu'il y a un car/un train à Bordeaux?

5 A quelle heure est-ce qu'il arrive/part?

6 Les trains pour Paris partent tous les combien, s'il vous plaît?

7 Je voudrais réserver une place.

8 J'ai réservé une place.

9 Où est la gare/la gare routière/la station de métro, s'il vous plaît?

10 Combien de temps dure le voyage?

11 Quand est le prochain vol?

12 Où est le guichet, s'il vous plaît?

13 Où est le bureau des renseignements, s'il vous plaît?

14 Où est la consigne/le bureau des objets trouvés, s'il vous plaît?

15 D'où part le train pour Paris, s'il vous plaît?

16 Le train pour Calais part de quel quai, s'il vous plaît?

17 Où est la station de taxis/l'arrêt d'autobus?

18 Est-ce qu'il y a une place de libre dans la voiture?

19 La place est occupée.

20 A quelle heure est-ce que l'avion décolle/atterrit?

21 Je voudrais prendre un taxi.

22 Où est-ce que je peux trouver un taxi?

23 Est-ce que le train est direct?

24 Est-ce qu'il faut changer?

25 Où est-ce qu'il faut changer?

26 Je voudrais un hôtel bon marché, s'il vous plaît.

27 Où est le buffet, s'il vous plaît?

28 A quelle heure part le prochain/le premier/le dernier car?

29 Je voudrais un compartiment non-fumeurs, s'il vous plaît.

30 Où est-ce que je peux déposer mes bagages, s'il vous plaît?

31 C'est le bon quai?

32 Où faut-il descendre?

33 Est-ce qu'il y a un wagon-restaurant/wagon-lit?

34 Est-ce qu'il y a une réduction/un supplément?

35 Où sont les toilettes, s'il vous plaît?

36 Où est la salle d'attente, s'il vous plaît?

37 Est-ce que je peux laisser mes bagages ici?

38 Est-ce que le vol est en retard?

39 Est-ce que le train est arrivé en avance?

40 J'ai perdu mon billet.

41 Combien coûte un carnet de tickets, s'il vous plaît?

42 Je voudrais un plan du métro, s'il vous plaît.

43 J'arriverai à vingt-deux heures.

44 Je partirai à deux heures du matin.

45 As-tu quelque chose à déclarer?

46 Je viens d'arriver.

47 Je prendrai le train de dix heures.

48 J'ai essayé de téléphoner de la gare.

49 Je téléphonerai de l'aéroport.

50 Où est-ce que je peux trouver un porteur?

51 Voulez-vous m'aider avec mes bagages?

52 J'ai manqué mon car.

53 Est-ce que le car va au centre-ville?

At the garage/filling station

1 Je voudrais vingt litres de super.

2 Donnez-moi dix litres de sans plomb.

3 Faites le plein, s'il vous plaît.

4 Voulez-vous vérifier l'huile, s'il vous plaît?

5 Voulez-vous vérifier la pression des pneus, s'il vous plaît?

6 Voulez-vous vérifier l'eau?

7 Où sont les toilettes, s'il vous plaît?

8 Vendez-vous les cartes routières, s'il vous plaît?

9 C'est bien la route pour Paris?

10 Pour aller à Toulouse?

11 La route de Paris est une route nationale ou une autoroute?

12 Où est-ce que nous pouvons stationner?

13 Notre voiture est en panne.

14 Je l'ai laissée à deux kilomètres d'ici.

15 Pouvez-vous nous aider?

16 Pouvez-vous réparer la voiture?

17 Il y a un mécanicien?

18 Les freins ne marchent pas.

19 J'ai un pneu crevé.

20 Une phare ne marche pas.

21 Le pare-brise est cassé.

22 J'ai besoin d'une batterie neuve.

23 Je vous dois combien?

24 Est-ce qu'on peut téléphoner d'ici?

25 Paris est à quelle distance d'ici?

26 Où est l'hôtel le plus proche, s'il vous plaît?

27 Vendez-vous des bonbons?

28 Voulez-vous nettoyer le pare-brise, s'il vous plaît?

29 Nous avons eu une panne d'essence.

30 Nous avons eu un accident.

31 Combien de temps faut-il attendre?

32 Ça va coûter combien?

At the customs

1 Je suis anglais(e)/irlandais(e)/écossais(e)/gallois(e).

2 Je n'ai rien à déclarer.

3 Je voudrais déclarer un appareil-photo.

4 J'ai deux valises et un sac.

5 La valise est à moi.

6 Il y a des vêtements et des cadeaux dans ma valise.

7 J'ai acheté la montre en Suisse il y a deux semaines.

8 Le parfum a coûté quatre cents francs.

9 Voulez-vous voir mon passeport?

10 Je serai en France pour deux semaines.

11 Je suis ici en vacances.

At the campsite

1 Je voudrais réserver un emplacement.

2 Est-ce que je peux camper ici?

3 Avez-vous de la place pour une tente?

4 J'ai une tente/caravane.

5 C'est combien pour une tente, deux adultes, quatre enfants et une voiture?

6 Je voudrais rester deux jours.

7 Je suis seul(e).

8 J'arriverai après-demain.

9 Je partirai samedi.

10 Où se trouve mon emplacement, s'il vous plaît?

11 Je voudrais un emplacement à l'ombre.

12 Je suis anglais(e)/irlandais(e)/écossais(e)/gallois(e).

13 Voulez-vous voir mon passeport?

14 Quand est-ce qu'il faut payer?

15 Je voudrais payer maintenant.

16 Pour aller au camping, s'il vous plaît?

17 Est-ce qu'il y a des douches chaudes?

18 Je voudrais un emplacement près du bloc sanitaire.

19 Où est-ce qu'il y a de l'eau potable?

20 Où est-ce qu'on peut faire la lessive/la vaisselle?

21 Quels sont les règlements?

22 Mon emplacement est trop près des poubelles.

23 Est-ce que je peux emprunter un ouvre-boîte/un tire-bouchon/
des allumettes?

24 Est-ce que je peux monter ma tente là-bas?

25 Où se trouve la prise de courant la plus proche?

26 C'est combien par personne?

27 C'est trop cher.

28 Est-ce qu'il y a une machine à laver ici?

29 Servez-vous des repas chauds?

30 Est-ce qu'il y a une épicerie ici?

31 Est-ce qu'on peut faire du feu?

32 Je suis très content(e) du camping.

33 Est-ce que le terrain de camping est bien équipé?

34 J'ai besoin d'une bouteille de gaz.

35 J'ai besoin de piles.

36 Est-ce que le terrain de camping est bien éclairé la nuit?

37 Est-ce que le terrain de camping est fermé la nuit?

38 Est-ce qu'il faut payer un supplément pour ça?

At the youth hostel

1 J'ai réservé un lit.

2 Je n'ai pas réservé un lit.

3 Est-ce qu'il y a des places de libres?

4 Est-ce qu'il y a un lit de libre?

5 Je partirai demain/après-demain.

6 Je resterai trois nuits.

7 Nous sommes deux garçons et deux jeunes filles.

8 Nous sommes anglais/irlandais/écossais/gallois.

9 C'est combien par personne par nuit?

10 Est-ce qu'il y a des magasins près d'ici?

11 Est-ce qu'il y a des douches, une cuisine, une salle de jeux?

12 Où sont les toilettes/les poubelles?

13 Je voudrais payer maintenant/plus tard/demain/en partant.

14 A quelle heure est-ce qu'on sert le petit déjeuner/le déjeuner/ le dîner?

15 A quelle heure est-ce que l'auberge est fermée?

16 A quelle heure est-ce que le bureau s'ouvre le matin?

17 Quels sont les règlements?

18 J'ai un sac de couchage.

19 Je voudrais louer un sac de couchage/des draps/des couvertures.

20 Où sont les dortoirs des jeunes filles et des garçons?

21 L'alcool est permis?

22 A quelle heure est-ce qu'on doit quitter l'auberge?

23 Est-ce qu'il faut remplir une fiche?

24 Est-ce qu'il y a de l'eau chaude?

25 Qu'est-ce qu'il faut faire avant de partir?

26 Où est-ce que je peux laisser mes objets de valeur?

27 J'ai une plainte.

28 Voulez-vous voir ma carte?

29 Est-ce que l'auberge est complète?

30 Est-ce que l'auberge est ouverte toute l'année?

31 Est-ce qu'on peut faire de la cuisine dans l'auberge?

32 Est-ce que vous servez des repas?

33 Pour aller à la salle à manger, s'il vous plaît?

34 Où est-ce que je peux laisser ma bicylette?

35 Je regrette mais je ne veux pas un lit en haut. Je voudrais un lit au rez-de-chaussée.

At the doctor's/
at the scene of an accident

1 Pouvez-vous m'aider, s'il vous plaît?

2 Voulez-vous téléphoner au médecin, s'il vous plaît?

3 Voulez-vous téléphoner pour une ambulance?

4 J'ai besoin d'un dentiste.

5 Je voudrais voir le médecin.

6 J'ai eu un accident.

7 J'ai mal aux dents.

8 J'ai mal à la gorge.

9 J'ai mal à la tête.

10 J'ai mal au ventre.

11 Je me suis cassé le bras/la jambe.

12 Il s'est cassé le bras/la jambe.

13 Je suis enrhumé(e).

14 Je me suis brûlé(e).

15 Je me suis brûlé le bras.

16 Il a une insolation/un coup de soleil.

17 Elle a la grippe.

18 Je me suis coupé(e).

19 Je me suis coupé la jambe.

20 Je suis tombé(e).

21 J'ai eu un accident de voiture.

22 J'ai de la fièvre.

23 J'ai le mal de mer.

24 Un insecte m'a piqué(e).

25 Je tousse.

26 J'ai vomi trois fois.

27 Mon ami est blessé.

28 Je dois revenir voir le médecin?

29 Je dois garder le lit?

30 J'ai besoin d'une ordonnance?

31 Où est la pharmacie, s'il vous plaît?

32 Je voudrais un reçu, s'il vous plaît.

33 Il faut prendre les comprimés pendant combien de temps?

34 Je voudrais acheter du coton hydrophile, un pansement, des sparadraps et de l'antiseptique.

35 Ma soeur se sent mal.

36 Je voudrais de l'asprine.

37 Deux heures/depuis hier.

38 Je dois prendre les comprimés tous les combien?

39 Je me sens mal/mieux.

40 Avez-vous quelque chose pour le mal de gorge?

41 Je ne prends aucun médicament.

42 J'ai une assurance.

43 Voulez-vous téléphoner à la police/aux pompiers?

44 L'accident a été grave.

45 Ce n'est pas de ma faute; c'est la faute de l'autre conducteur.

46 Avez-vous une crème pour les coups de soleil?

47 Mon père a freiné mais il y a eu une collision.

48 Le moteur a pris feu.

49 Le permis de conduire de mon père est à l'hôtel.

50 Un cycliste a renversé un vieillard qui traversait la rue.

51 Ça me fait mal.

Shopping for food and drink

1 Je voudrais un pain, s'il vous plaît.

2 C'est combien?

3 Je voudrais acheter des gâteaux.

4 Cinq cents grammes de jambon, s'il vous plaît.

5 Je voudrais du boeuf/du mouton/du lapin.

6 Deux cent cinquante grammes de saucisse, s'il vous plaît.

7 Est-ce qu'il y a une épicerie ouverte près d'ici?

8 Je voudrais acheter des cigarettes pour mon père.

9 Deux cents grammes de cerises/de bananes/d'oranges/de pêches/de poires/de pommes/de fraises/d'abricots/de raisins, s'il vous plaît.

10 Je voudrais un ananas/un melon.

11 Où est-ce que je peux acheter des légumes?

12 Donnez-moi une livre de haricots verts/d'oignons/de petits pois/ de pommes de terre/de champignons/de chou/de carrottes/ de chou-fleur.

13 Une laitue, s'il vous plaît.

14 Est-ce qu'il y a une boucherie près d'ici?

15 Je voudrais un kilo de poulet/de lapin/de boeuf.

16 Est-ce que la viande est bonne dans ce magasin?

17 Où est-ce que je peux acheter des fruits de mer?

18 Une livre de saucisse/de pâté.

19 Je voudrais deux litres de vin rouge et un litre de vin blanc.

20 Cinq litres de bière, s'il vous plaît.

21 Un pot de café, s'il vous plaît.

22 Une bouteille d'eau minérale, s'il vous plaît.

23 Je voudrais du jus de fruit, s'il vous plaît.

24 Deux litres de lait, s'il vous plaît.

25 Un paquet de thé, s'il vous plaît.

26 Une douzaine d'oeufs, s'il vous plaît.

27 Où est-ce que je peux acheter du sel/du poivre?

28 Une tranche de fromage, s'il vous plaît.

29 J'achète de la nourriture pour un pique-nique.

30 Deux cents grammes de beurre, s'il vous plaît.

31 Est-ce que vous vendez des bonbons/du chocolat?

32 Je voudrais un paquet de sucre, s'il vous plaît.

33 Je ne l'aime pas. Je ne vais pas le prendre.

34 C'est trop cher.

35 Vous m'en avez donné trop/trop peu.

36 Je le prends.

37 C'est tout.

38 Combien je vous dois, s'il vous plaît?

39 Je voudrais de la monnaie.

40 J'ai acheté ce fromage ici. Il n'est pas bon. Voulez-vous me rendre mon argent, s'il vous plaît.

41 Je n'ai qu'un billet de cent francs.

42 Est-ce que je peux choisir le fruit que je veux?

43 Un peu plus grand, s'il vous plaît.

44 Avez-vous quelque chose de moins cher?

45 Où est la caisse, s'il vous plaît?

46 Je voudrais une boîte en carton/un sac en plastique.

47 Est-ce que je peux payer avec un chèque ou une carte de crédit?

48 Est-ce que vous êtes ouvert dimanche?

49 A quelle heure est-ce que vous ouvrez/fermez?

Shopping for clothes and toiletries

1 C'est quelle taille, s'il vous plaît?

2 C'est quelle pointure, s'il vous plaît?

3 Est-ce que la chemise est en coton/en nylon?

4 Est-ce que le pull est en laine?

5 Je voudrais acheter des pantoufles.

6 Est-ce que les gants sont en cuir?

7 J'aime ce blouson/cette veste.

8 Où sont les cabines d'essayage, s'il vous plaît?

9 Je voudrais essayer ce pantalon.

10 Avez-vous la même jupe en bleu?

11 La robe et trop longue/courte/étroite/large/grande/petite.

12 Voulez-vous me faire un paquet-cadeau pour l'écharpe?

13 Pour aller au rayon des hommes, s'il vous plaît?

14 Pour aller à la caisse, s'il vous plaît?

15 Où est l'ascenseur/la sortie?

16 A quelle heure est-ce que vous fermez/ouvrez?

17 Est-ce que je peux écouter ce disque?

18 Je voudrais un sac en plastique, s'il vous plaît.

19 Est-ce que je peux échanger ce manteau?

20 Ce n'est pas la bonne taille.

21 Est-ce qu'il y a un autre magasin qui vend des pulls?

22 Vous vous êtes trompé(e).

23 Qu'est-ce que tu vas acheter?

24 Est-ce que ce tee-shirt me va?

25 Où est-ce que je peux acheter du savon/du shampooing/un peigne/une brosse à dents/du dentifrice?

26 Je voudrais faire du lèche-vitrines.

27 C'est trop cher.

28 C'est très bon marché.

29 Avez-vous ma taille?

30 Avez-vous quelque chose de moins cher?

31 Où est-ce qu'il faut payer?

At the cleaner's/launderette

1 Pouvez-vous nettoyer ce pantalon, s'il vous plaît?

2 Pouvez-vous raccommoder ce chemisier, s'il vous plaît?

3 Il faudra combien de temps, s'il vous plaît?

4 Je voudrais laver ces vêtements.

5 Avez-vous de la monnaie pour la machine à laver?

6 J'ai besoin de quelles pièces pour la machine à laver?

7 Où est-ce que je peux acheter de la lessive?

At the café/restaurant

1 Garçon/mademoiselle/madame. Le menu, s'il vous plaît.

2 Je voudrais laisser un pourboire.

3 Je voudrais réserver une table.

4 J'ai réservé une table.

5 Une tasse/une soucoupe/un couteau/une fourchette/une cuillère/un verre, s'il vous plaît.

6 La nappe est sale.

7 Je voudrais commander.

8 Voulez-vous enlever le plateau?

9 L'addition, s'il vous plaît.

10 Santé! Bon appétit!

11 Voulez-vous choisir le vin?

12 Où est le téléphone/Où sont les toilettes, s'il vous plaît?

13 Est-ce que le service est compris?

14 J'ai faim/soif.

15 Je voudrais le steak saignant/à point/bien cuit.

16 Le repas est délicieux.

17 Qu'est-ce que vous voulez prendre comme dessert?

18 Je me sens mal.

19 Je voudrais le menu à quatre-vingts francs.

20 Je voudrais le plat du jour.

21 Je voudrais une côte de porc avec oignons, petits pois et frites.

22 Est-ce que vous servez le petit déjeuner?

23 Je voudrais un café/un café crème.

24 Je voudrais de la soupe, du lapin, du riz/des pommes de terre.

25 Je voudrais un sandwich au fromage/pâté/jambon.

26 Je voudrais des huîtres/des moules.

27 Je voudrais de la truite/des sardines.

28 Je voudrais du concombre dans la salade.

29 Je voudrais des cérises/une banane/un melon/une orange/
une pêche/une poire/une pomme/des fraises/des abricots/de
l'ananas/des raisins.

30 Je voudrais du poulet, des haricots verts, des champignons et des
carottes.

31 Je n'aime pas le chou.

32 Le chou-fleur n'est pas bon.

33 Est-ce qu'il y a de l'agneau?

34 Quelles boissons servez-vous?

35 Je voudrais un litre de vin blanc/rouge.

36 Je voudrais un bière.

37 Je voudrais un jus de fruit/de l'eau minérale/du lait/du thé.

38 Je voudrais un oeuf à la coque/sur le plat/poché/brouillé.

39 Du sel/du poivre/du vinaigre/de la moutarde, s'il vous plaît.

40 Une tranche de jambon, s'il vous plaît.

41 Voulez-vous nettoyer la table?

42 Je voudrais être à la terrasse au soleil/à l'ombre.

43 Je voudrais une table pour deux personnes près de la fenêtre.

44 Vous avez fait une erreur.

45 Je ne comprends pas le menu. Qu'est-ce que c'est ce plat?

46 Voulez-vous fermer/ouvrir la fenêtre?

47 J'en voudrais encore, s'il vous plaît.

48 Je voudrais un cendrier, s'il vous plaît.

49 Vous avez oublié la glace à la vanille.

50 Je voudrais de la monnaie pour le téléphone, s'il vous plaît.

51 La nourriture est froide.

52 Ma fourchette est sale.

53 Je voudrais quelque chose de frais/de chaud à boire.

54 J'ai trop chaud/froid.

55 Je n'ai pris qu'une limonade et un jus d'orange.

56 Voulez-vous vérifier l'addition?

57 Je suis pressé(e). Ça va prendre combien de temps?

58 Nous sommes quatre.

59 Ce plat est du poisson, pas de la viande.

60 Acceptez-vous les cartes de crédit?

61 Je n'ai pas commandé de vin.

62 Est-ce qu'il y a un choix de légumes?

63 Ça sent bon.

64 As-tu décidé?

65 C'est trop cher.

66 Quel vin veux-tu?

At the post office

1 Où est le bureau de poste, s'il vous plaît?

2 Est-ce qu'il y a une boîte aux lettres ici?

3 C'est combien pour envoyer une lettre/carte postale en Angleterre?

4 Je voudrais envoyer une lettre en Grande-Bretagne.

5 Je voudrais envoyer un colis.

6 Est-ce qu'il y a un paquet ici pour moi?

7 Je voudrais deux timbres à cinq francs.

8 A quelle heure est-ce que vous ouvrez/fermez?

9 Est-ce qu'il y a une lettre pour moi au guichet poste restante?

10 Est-ce qu'il y a une cabine téléphonique ici?

11 J'ai besoin de pièces pour téléphoner au Royaume Uni.

12 Je voudrais envoyer un télégramme.

13 C'est combien pour envoyer un télégramme?

14 Une lettre arrivera en Grande-Bretagne après combien de temps?

15 Est-ce qu'il y a une boîte spéciale pour les lettres à l'étranger?

16 Où est-ce que je peux poster cette lettre?

17 Je voudrais téléphoner en Angleterre.

18 Je voudrais acheter un mandat.

19 C'est à quel guichet, s'il vous plaît?

20 Je voudrais envoyer la lettre par avion.

21 Est-ce qu'il faut remplir un formulaire?

22 Est-ce que le bureau de poste est ouvert le samedi?

23 Est-ce qu'il y a un service plus rapide?

24 Quand est la prochaine levée?

On the telephone

1 Où est le téléphone le plus proche, s'il vous plaît?

2 Puis-je voir l'annuaire, s'il vous plaît?

3 Est-ce que je peux parler avec Jean?

4 Je n'entends pas la tonalité.

5 Voulez-vous me donner le numéro de téléphone du syndicat d'initiative, s'il vous plaît?

6 Je voudrais parler avec l'opératrice.

7 Je voudrais faire un PCV.

8 Allô. C'est Melanie à l'appareil.

9 Voulez-vous laisser un mot?

10 Je ne vous entends pas. Voulez-vous parler moins vite?

11 Ne quittez pas.

12 Je me suis trompé(e) de numéro.

At the bank/exchange office

1 Où est-ce qu'il faut faire la queue?

2 Je voudrais changer des livres en francs.

3 Je voudrais changer des chèques de voyage en francs.

4 C'est quel guichet, s'il vous plaît?

5 C'est mon tour?

6 Quel est le cours du change, s'il vous plaît?

7 Voulez-vous voir mon passeport?

8 J'ai oublié mon passeport.

9 Je vais chercher mon passeport.

10 Où est-ce qu'il faut signer?

11 Combien vaut la livre?

12 Est-ce qu'il faut passer à la caisse?

13 J'ai une carte de crédit.

14 J'ai une carte bancaire.

15 Est-ce qu'il faut payer une commission?

16 Est-ce que vous prenez dix pour cent pour la commission?

17 Je voudrais des billets de cent francs.

18 Je voudrais des pièces de dix francs.

19 On m'a volé tout mon argent.

20 Voulez-vous téléphoner à ma banque en Angleterre?

21 Voulez-vous demander à ma banque d'envoyer de l'argent?

At the police station/ lost-property office

1 J'ai perdu quelque chose. Où est le commissariat de police, s'il vous plaît?

2 J'ai trouvé quelque chose. Où est le bureau des objets trouvés, s'il vous plaît?

3 L'appareil-photo est assez grand.

4 Je ne sais pas la marque.

5 Je l'ai acheté il y a deux ans.

6 Il y a cinq ans que je l'ai.

7 Il vaut cent livres.

8 La valise contenait des vêtements, une montre et une bague d'or.

9 Le porte-monnaie contenait vingt livres.

10 Le portefeuille contenait mille francs.

11 Je n'ai pas vu le voleur/cambrioleur.

12 Je l'ai perdu devant le guichet.

13 Je l'ai laissé dans ma chambre.

14 La valise était dans la voiture de mon père.

15 Je l'ai perdu il y a deux heures/hier/avant-hier.

16 Est-ce qu'on a trouvé la bague?

17 Je suis un(e) touriste britannique.

18 Le sac à main est à ma soeur.

19 L'appareil-photo est à moi.

20 Est-ce qu'il faut payer?

21 Qu' est-ce qu'il faut faire maintenant?

22 Je reviendrai demain.

23 J'écrirai.

24 Je téléphonerai.

25 On nous a volé la voiture.

26 On a volé beaucoup de choses de notre voiture.

27 J'ai perdu mes chèques de voyage/mon passeport.

28 Est-ce que je peux emprunter de l'argent?

29 Voulez-vous me prêter de l'argent?

30 Le voleur s'est sauvé.

31 C'est un cadeau de ma tante.

32 Je suis très fâché(e)/déçu(e)/surpris(e)/content(e).

At the tourist information office

1 Je suis un(e) touriste britannique.

2 Avez-vous des renseignements sur la région?

3 Avez-vous des brochures?

4 Avez-vous un plan de la ville?

5 Avez-vous une carte de la région?

6 Avez-vous l'horaire des autobus?

7 Avez-vous une liste des hôtels et des terrains de camping?

8 Quels sont les lieux d'intérêt?

9 Avez-vous des renseignements sur le château?

10 Je voudrais des renseignements sur le musée.

11 Est-ce qu'il y a des excursions à faire?

12 Qu'est-ce qu'il y a à faire le soir?

13 Est-ce qu'il y a des spectacles/distractions?

14 A quelle heure est-ce que le musée ouvre/ferme?

15 J'aime le sport. Est-ce qu'il y a des facilités?

16 Est-ce qu'on peut louer des skis/une bicyclette?

17 Est-ce qu'on peut acheter les billets ici?

18 Est-ce qu'il y a un cirque/théâtre/concert dans la région?

19 Je m'intéresse aux châteaux.

Asking the way

1 Pardon, monsieur/madame/mademoiselle.

2 Je suis perdu(e).

3 Pour aller au centre-ville, s'il vous plaît?

4 C'est loin?

5 C'est à quelle distance?

6 Tournez à droite au carrefour.

7 Tournez à gauche après la banque.

8 Traversez le pont et allez tout droit.

9 Montez la rue jusqu'au supermarché.

10 Descendez la rue jusqu'au feu rouge.

11 C'est en face du cinéma.

12 Suivez la route jusqu'au rond-point.

13 L'arrêt d'autobus est à gauche.

14 Prenez la première rue à droite.

15 Prenez la deuxième rue après l'arrêt d'autobus.

16 Allez tout droit jusqu'au coin de la rue.

17 Avez-vous une carte routière/un plan de la ville?

18 Prenez l'autoroute, monsieur/madame/mademoiselle.

19 Je ne connais pas la région.

20 C'est à cinq kilomètres d'ici.

21 C'est à cinq minutes d'ici à pied.

22 Prenez un taxi/le métro/l'autobus, monsieur/madame/
mademoiselle.

23 C'est derrière la boulangerie.

24 Quel est le numéro de l'autobus?

25 Je vous accompagnerai.

26 Descendez le couloir et prenez l'ascenseur au premier étage.

27 Je ne comprends pas.

28 Voulez-vous répétez cela, s'il vous plaît?

29 Où est-ce que je peux trouver un taxi?

At the cinema

1 Qu'est-ce qu'on joue au cinéma?

2 Est-ce que le film a des sous-titres?

3 C'est en version française?

4 Je voudrais réserver deux places.

5 Veux-tu aller au cinéma ce soir?

6 Est-ce qu'il faut donner un pourboire à l'ouvreuse?

7 A quelle heure est-ce que le film commence?

8 A quelle heure est-ce que le film finit?

9 Est-ce qu'il y a un entracte?

10 Combien coûte une place au balcon?

11 Je voudrais une place à l'orchestre.

12 Le film m'a plu.

13 Le film ne m'a pas plu.

14 Est-ce qu'il y a une réduction pour les groupes?

15 Je préfère les films policiers.

16 Si on se rencontre devant le cinéma?

17 C'est quelle sorte de film?

18 Je ne suis pas d'accord.

19 Est-ce que le film t'a plu?

20 Je suis d'accord.

At the hotel

1 Je voudrais réserver une chambre.

2 J'ai réservé une chambre.

3 Je voudrais une chambre pour une personne.

4 Je voudrais une chambre pour deux personnes.

5 Je voudrais une chambre avec un lit d'une personne.

6 Je voudrais une chambre avec un lit de deux personnes.

7 Je voudrais une chambre avec deux lits d'une personne.

8 Je voudrais une chambre de famille.

9 Avez-vous une chambre avec douche ou une salle de bain?

10 Je resterai pour quatre nuits.

11 Je voudrais partir demain matin.

12 Je voudrais partir de très bon matin.

13 Je voudrais une chambre au rez-de-chausée.

14 Ma chambre se trouve à quel étage, s'il vous plaît?

15 Ma chambre est quel numéro?

16 Est-ce que vous servez des repas?

17 A quelle heure est-ce qu'on sert le petit déjeuner?

18 Est-ce que le petit déjeuner est compris?

19 Avez-vous des chambres de libres?

20 Je suis anglais(e)/irlandais(e)/écossais(e)/gallois(e).

21 Est-ce qu'il faut remplir une fiche?

22 Voulez-vous me donner ma clé, s'il vous plaît?

23 La note, s'il vous plaît.

24 La note n'est pas correcte.

25 Je voudrais payer par chèque ou par carte de crédit.

26 Est-ce qu'il y a un cinéma près d'ici?

27 Pour aller à la salle à manger, s'il vous plaît?

28 Il n'y a pas de savon dans ma chambre.

29 Je voudrais encore un oreiller, s'il vous plaît.

30 Je ne suis pas satisfait(e) de ma chambre. Voulez-vous téléphoner à un autre hôtel?

31 Je voudrais me plaindre.

32 Il n'y a pas de serviette dans ma chambre.

33 J'ai perdu ma clef.

34 Avez-vous quelque chose de moins cher?

35 Est-ce que nous pouvons monter nos bagages maintenant?

36 Est-ce qu'il y a un parking près d'ici?

37 Je voudrais une chambre qui donne sur la plage.

38 Nous prendrons ces chambres.

39 J'ai réservé une chambre par téléphone.

40 L'ascenseur ne marche pas.

41 Je voudrais encore des cintres.

42 Le robinet a une fuite.

43 La lampe ne marche pas.

44 Le lavabo est bouché.

45 Il y a trop de bruit dans ma chambre.

46 Je voudrais une autre chambre.

47 Je suis très déçu(e).

48 Je voudrais encore une couverture, s'il vous plaît.

Visiting and receiving an exchange partner

1 Enchanté(e).

2 Bienvenue!

3 Je te présente mon frère.

4 C'est un cadeau de mes parents.

5 J'ai un frère et deux soeurs.

6 Où est ma chambre/la salle de bains?

7 Je te ferai voir ta chambre.

8 La salle de bains est en haut, à gauche.

9 Je voudrais téléphoner à mes parents.

10 Veux-tu téléphoner à tes parents?

11 A quelle heure est le petit déjeuner?

12 Le petit déjeuner est à huit heures.

13 Je suis fatigué(e). Je voudrais me coucher.

14 Es-tu fatigué(e)?

15 Est-ce que tu veux te coucher?

16 Le voyage a été très fatigant.

17 J'aime la cuisine française.

18 Est-ce que tu aimes la cuisine anglaise?

19 Je n'aime pas le chou.

20 Est-ce qu'il y a des plats que tu n'aimes pas?

21 A quelle heure est-ce qu'on part demain?

22 Où est-ce que je peux mettre mes vêtements?

23 Où est-ce que je peux mettre ma valise?

24 Où est-ce qu'on peut se rencontrer?

25 Je voudrais connaître tes amis.

26 Veux-tu connaître mes amis?

27 Est-ce qu'il y a quelque chose que tu veux faire?

28 Qu'est-ce que tu veux faire?

29 Je voudrais sortir.

30 Je voudrais aller à la plage.

31 Si on se rencontrait devant la gare?

32 Je suis grand(e)/petit(e).

33 Je porte des lunettes.

34 J'ai les cheveux courts/longs.

35 J'ai les cheveux frisés/raides.

36 J'ai les cheveux bruns/noirs/blonds.

37 Je porterai un pardessus/un manteau vert et un jean.

38 Je me sens mal.

39 Je me suis fait mal.

40 Qu'est-ce que tu porteras?

41 Es-tu malade?

42 Est-ce que tu t'es fait mal?

43 Où est-ce que je peux laver mes vêtements sales?

44 As-tu des vêtements sales?

45 Est-ce que je peux regarder la télévision?

46 Est-ce que tu veux regarder la télévision?

47 Je voudrais aider ta mère.

48 Je vais mettre/débarrasser la table.

49 Je voudrais faire la vaisselle.

50 Je voudrais aller à la boum.

51 Est-ce que tu veux aller à la boum?

52 Comment pourrons-nous rentrer de la ville?

53 Nous pourrons rentrer en car.

54 Je ne veux pas partager une chambre.

55 As-tu du savon/une serviette/du dentifrice?

56 J'ai besoin d'un savon/d'une serviette/d'un tube de dentifrice.

57 Est-ce que tu voudrais prendre un bain/une douche?

58 Je voudrais prendre un bain/une douche.

59 J'ai faim/soif/chaud/froid.

60 Je voudrais me reposer.

61 Je voudrais emprunter de l'argent.